Persistence of Vision

By: Nike Binger Marshall

Persistence of Vision

By: Nike Binger Marshall

Cover Design By: Anelda Ballard

Logo Design By: Andre M. Saunders

Editor: Anelda Ballard

Contributing Artist: Kayla Stern

Photographs By: www.photobucket.com and www.inmagine.com

© 2009 Nike Binger Marshall

ISBN 978-0-9843255-1-1

ISBN 0-9843255-1-4

All rights reserved. This book is protected under the copyright laws of the United States of America. This book may not be copied or reprinted for commercial gain or profit. The use of short quotations or occasional page copying for personal or group study is permitted and encouraged. Permission will be granted on request.

For Worldwide Distribution. Printed in the United States of America

Published by Jazzy Kitty Greetings Marketing & Publishing, LLC

Using Microsoft Publishing Software.

ACKNOWLEDGMENTS

I can do nothing without God. This book is evidence of a promise He made to me many years ago. I understand the responsibility that comes with the promise and I thank Him for this gift that He has given me.

On my journey to publishing this book, God has placed people in my life that gave me the push and the confidence to bring this work to fruition. Sharon Josey, thank you for giving me the push I needed to stand on stage and read my work. It was uncomfortable, but I really needed to come out of my poetic closet. Thank you for also being an extra pair of eyes and assisting with the editing of this book. Your new nickname is "Eagle-Eye Josey." New Genesis, I really love you all. Thank you for your prayers and encouragement. I thank God for each and every one of you! Simpson United Methodist Church, you are the best extended family a girl could ever have! I'm glad to have grown spiritually with you. You represent Christ well. Everyone should experience this kind of love, support and encouragement. Secluded Paradise 2, you all have taught me where to find the words. You have stretched me and brought things out in me that I didn't know were there. What you do is absolutely amazing! Don't be discouraged when things seem to slow down. What you do for poetry is absolutely valuable! Ronald and Anelda Ballard, God uses who He chooses or so I've heard! Thank you for taking on this project. I did not think publishing a book would be easy, but with you it has been a breeze! Kayla Stern, I am so proud of you! Your talent is amazing. Thank you for being willing to contribute artwork to my book. I know you will go far!

To my family: You all can be tough sometimes, but I thank you for helping me develop a thick skin and for being supportive and encouraging upon hearing about this project. It truly means the world to me.

DEDICATION

To Zeni,

One part vision + A little persistence = Dream come true.

TABLE OF CONTENTS

Introduction..	i
Be the Promise...	02
Missing You..	04
Dad..	06
I Dream...	08
Eulogy...	10
Dear Poet..	12
I Am...	14
I Gotta Write...	16
Let It Slip...	18
I Love You Enough..	19
Kept...	21
Motherly Advice...	23
Move Me...	26
My Only Need..	29
Paint Myself Gold..	31
Persistence of Vision..	34
Right Here..	36
Roses and Thorns (Benedita da Silva).....................................	38
Oasis..	40

TABLE OF CONTENTS

Satisfaction	42
She	43
Sustain	46
Testimony	48
The Dream is Yet Alive	50
The Measure of an Artist	51
What You See Before You	53
You Are Nobody	54
About the Author	56
Contributing Artist	57
Persistence of Vision Telecom Definition	58

INTRODUCTION

"When did you become a poet?" I recently saw this question on a blog and began to consider my journey to this place. Writing has been my "thing" for as long as I can remember. I discovered writing when I about 6 years old. A group came to our school and taught us how to write haiku. I wrote something deep and profound in those three little lines. The instructors thought it was great as well as the other pieces my classmates wrote. A few weeks later, they came back and handed out mustard colored paperback books to the class. The haiku written by my class, poetry and artwork of other students were all contained in that book. I didn't know little kids could create a book! It absolutely blew my six year old mind! I continued to write throughout Junior High and High School mostly as an outlet. I was raised in a very strict household where children were seen and not heard. Writing was the only way that I could clearly and freely express myself.

I put writing aside following the birth of my daughter and as many women do, I chose to focus on family needs, which meant putting aside my desire to write. As happy as I was to be a new mom, I felt like I gave up a huge piece of myself. I don't recall who said it, but I heard a quote once that said something like, *if you wake up each day and can only think about writing, then you are a writer.* That quote entered my mind many times during the years that I was not writing. About five years ago, I decided to "get me back." I picked

INTRODUCTION

up my pen and started writing poetry and began to feel whole again. I was a happier person, but didn't consider myself a poet at that point.

As long as I was writing for myself, I could only consider myself an avid journal keeper. I did not believe I could be considered a poet until I took the risk of sharing my work with others. I started by sharing my poetry in blogs and received great feedback and encouragement from other writers. Then I took the greater risk of sharing my work with family and friends. It's one thing to receive negative feedback from a stranger, I don't have to encounter a stranger on a daily basis, but opening myself up to friends and family was one of the hardest things I've ever done. Family and friends can be tough critics at times, so when my family gave me praise and encouragement for my work, I was thrilled!

Now that I've done the hard thing, sharing my work with my cozy network of online friends as well as with family, I've decided to put a few of my poems together in a book and present this gift to you. I'm expanding my boundaries!

BE THE PROMISE

10 GENERATIONS, 400 YEARS.

THEY DIED WITHOUT THEIR GIVEN NAMES.

THEY LAY HIDDEN IN UNMARKED GRAVES,

IN SIMPLE PINE BOXES, IN ABANDONED PLOTS

SHROUDED BY WEEDS AND OVER GROWN TREES

BE THE PROMISE

10 Generations, 400 Years.

We don't know how to live anymore.

We don't recognize God and He knows us not.

Our house is out of order, built on a sandy cliff.

We live day by day, standing at a distance,

far from each other and even farther from God.

10 Generations, 400 Years.

We don't know how to fight anymore.

We don't recognize the enemy

because we've become comfortable

in the garment of success.

We know nothing of barely enough.

We have forgotten the joy in going without

and being content not realizing anything was ever missing.

10 Generations, 400 Years.

We don't know how to die anymore.

Our home goings are an elaborate illusion of a life well lived.

We lie about our living and giving

and rob each other by not extending our hands

and spreading our fingers to one another.

We slumber with false accolades chiseled

In monuments that mark our places of rest.

(Continued)

BE THE PROMISE

10 Generations, 400 Years.
They died without their given names.
They lay hidden in unmarked graves,
in simple pine boxes, in abandoned plots,
shrouded by weeds and over grown trees.
They lived without,
gave all they had, even their lives
so The Promise would not starve.
They fought every battle,
so The Promise would not perish.
They died tending to The Promise
so it would become fruitful.

10 Generations, 400 Years.
They knew from the beginning,
we were born a threat
They did not die
to become history or legends or mythology.
They lived, they fought, they labored, they died,
so the threat could become The Promise.

10 Generations, 400 Years.
Be The Promise.

MISSING YOU

My eyes search up high
Seeking the light in darkness,
looking past the stars.

How I wish to see your face.
How I wish to touch your face

DAD

Caroll C. Young

HE PUT HIMSELF IN DANGER'S PATH
WHEN HE TAUGHT ME HOW TO DRIVE.
HE SHOWED ME HOW TO PAY MY BILLS,
LOVE THE LORD AND TESTIFY.

(In memory of C. Young)

DAD

He taught me how to ride a bike
and babysat my dolls,
He played tea party, he played house,
he protected me from harm.

He put himself in danger's path
when he taught me how to drive.
He showed me how to pay my bills,
love the Lord and testify.

A smile would spread upon his face
when he saw his children win.
He planted seeds in our lives
to shield our souls from sin.

As we grew and birthed our own,
he stood like a redwood tree.
He held these brand new lives in his hands
and spoke blessing over each Legacy.

Daily we honor his walk in life
by the things we do and say;
to spread a bit of his light and love,
to those we meet each day.

(In memory of C. Young)

I DREAM
(Dream Dreamer)

"Dream as if you'll live forever, live as if you'll die today."
James Dean (American motion picture actor, 1931-1955)

"What is not started today is never finished tomorrow."
Johann Wolfgang von Goethe
(GERMAN PLAYWRIGHT, POET,
NOVELIST AND DRAMATIST. 1749-1832)

I DREAM
(Dream Dreamer)

Dream Dreamer! Dream as if you'll live forever!

Dream in color and let the lines reach,

beyond the horizon and pierce the heart of the sun.

Don't move like a rolling mist,

across the dew kissed fields,

but run to your vision like the fearsome lion,

pursuing his prey.

Every moment live as if you'll die today.

Dream! Dreamer, dream!

Don't wait for the perfect time.

For what is not started today

is never finished tomorrow.

Don't you know that dreams have wings,

to carry you over mountain peaks,

or pass you by in pursuit of a more passionate mate?

Therefore Dreamer, dream.

Dream.

EULOGY

I CRIED A STEADY STREAM OF SALTY TEARS.
SOOTHING WORDS COULD NOT
PENETRATE MY PAIN.
THEY WOULDN'T LET ME TOUCH MY SON.

EULOGY

He was a good son,
well mannered and on his way to being a man;
never known to run the streets,
or seen with the wrong crowd.

Yet, there he lay,
the groceries scattered on his left,
his right hand outstretched.
The list I gave him: milk, juice, bread, eggs, aspirin,
lay crumbled near his open hand.

His bloodshot eyes stared at me, full of alarm.
The last word he screamed, "NO!"
seemed to linger on his twisted lips.

His life painted the pavement red.
The wail of the siren blended with my screams.
Words of comfort swirled around me.
I cried a steady stream of salty tears.
Soothing words could not penetrate my pain.

(Continued)

EULOGY

They wouldn't let me touch my son.

My son.

I needed to hold him again.

I wanted to pick his life up and pour it back into him,

even give him my own,

if it would bring him back.

I needed him to take a breath

and call to me, "Mom," just one more time.

I'd give him my own breath to make it happen.

Through my pain, I know another mother will suffer when She

discovers her son is a murderer.

I forgive him, but I pray that his mother will never feel,

The pain I am feeling now.

DEAR POET

I could spend forever, between your lines,
gleaning joy and happiness,
love and passion,

feeling your pulse, when you are sad,
or angry, or frustrated.
I'll caress your heart, by reading your words.

Do you feel me feeling what you feel?
Do you feel my feelings,
wanting to keep you in a place of peace
instead of leaving you stranded on a sheet of paper
dear Poet?

I AM

I AM THE LIFE YOU WISH YOU COULD LIVE.

I AM THE LOVE YOU WILL NEVER KNOW.

I AM

"I am the miracle."

Buddha-Hindu Prince Gautama Siddharta, 563-483 B.C.

I am the miracle, you left for dead,
the hope for the future you tried to kill

I am the rose that grew in concrete.
I am the success you could never achieve.
I am the life you wish you could live.
I am the love you will never know.
I am more than the survivor you tried to slay.

I am the fear in your eyes,
the trembling in your heart,
the quivering in your gut.

The secret you want forever quieted.
I am the conqueror of your inflicted pain.

I AM HERE.

I GOTTA WRITE

I NEED MORE WORDS

WHERE ARE THE WORDS??!!

THEY CAN'T RUN OUT!!

I NEED TO...

I GOTTA WRITE

I gotta write

I gotta write

Can't stop

I'll suffocate

I have to write

Tell a story

I need more ink

My life depends on it

I must write

I must write

Lines on a page can't contain me

I need to write

You need to hear

You need to read

Tell me what you think

The lack of feedback will kill me.

I need more words

Where are the words??!!

They can't run out!!

I need to…

I LET IT SLIP

I LET IT SLIP ONE DAY, THOSE 3 LITTLE WORDS
I LOVE YOU
I COULDN'T TAKE THEM BACK
THEY JUST HUNG IN THE AIR
LIKE A FLASHING NEON SIGN.

I LET IT SLIP

I let it slip one day, those 3 little words

I   Love   You

I couldn't take them back.

They just hung in the air

like a flashing neon sign.

I let it slip one day, those 3 little words

I   Need   You

I couldn't take them back.

I obligated myself.

I relinquished my freedom.

I let it slip one day, those 3 little words

I   Hate   You

I wouldn't take them back.

I killed you with those words

and with the same words, committed verbal suicide.

I let it loose one day, those 3 little words

I   Forgive   You

I let them stand on their own;

erase the words I spoke before

and was restored with life anew.

I LOVE YOU ENOUGH

I love you enough to tell you the truth.
Know that the things I say and feel are true.
I call you mine, but know you're not.
I love you enough to overlook that fact
and accept that you walk in
and out of my life freely.

You embody all of the wonderful things
this universe has to offer
and I love you enough to embrace them all.

I love you enough to tell you:
I need more...I want more.

I love you enough not to make demands
or give you ultimatums
because I respect your freedom.

(Continued)

I LOVE YOU ENOUGH

I love you enough to tell you

I don't want a part-time love.

Do you love me enough to meet my needs?

Do you love me enough to admit that you can't?

I love myself enough to walk away from this love

before the realities of life

destroy the memories we shared.

KEPT

I want to be kept.

It is nice to be wanted.

But after awhile,

I know it is not enough.

We feel so temporary.

Can I be more than wanted?

MOTHERLY ADVICE

LET LOVE BE YOUR RESCUER
AND NOT THE LIKES OF MEN.
**IF YOU BLINDLY GIVE YOUR LOVE,
YOUR HEART WILL BREAK AGAIN.**

MOTHERLY ADVICE

I see the pain in your eyes
and I don't understand
why you give up so much
and he has empty hands.

Oh, yes he is quite handsome,
the funds he makes seem fine,
but what good are those things
if his heart is so unkind?

He withholds his affection,
he withholds all his time.
He lives by the mantra:
"What's yours is mine and what's mine is mine."

I was once like you, Dear Child
both hands open, always giving,
dying day by day inside,
swallowing bitterness, never living.

(Continued)

MOTHERLY ADVICE

There's balance in love, Dear Child;
at times there's joy, at times there's sadness,
and there are calm times and passion too,
but most often there is gladness.

Let love be your rescuer
and not the likes of men.
If you blindly give your love,
your heart will break again.

That your joy be sweet like flowing honey,
is my hope for your tomorrow.
I pray you will drink the sweetness of love,
and nevermore swallow sorrow.

MOVE ME

BEFORE YOU APPROACH ME,

WITH SILVER TONGUED PHRASES

PLAY WITH MY HEART AND PUT ME THROUGH PACES

ANSWER THE QUESTION MAN:

CAN YOU MOVE ME?

MOVE ME

Don't tell me about my eyes
Don't tell me about my lips
Don't tell me about my hair
Don't tell me about my hips
Move me.

Don't tell me that I'm fly,
the prettiest thing you've seen in while
Man, I know I'm fine!
Brother, move me!

Talk is cheap
Kisses aren't always sweet
Move me brother, move me!

Tell me about your history
Where have you been?
Where are you going?
Show me how you love,
Show me how you share
How do you give?
How do you live?
Man, move me.

(Continued)

MOVE ME

Show me God in your life,

Show me you know how to fight

Not with gun or fist or knife,

But with bowed head and clasped hands.

Tell me, can you move me man?

You don't need to touch me

To make me feel good

Pleasing my body comes second

To feeding my heart and soul.

Pricey gifts and fancy trips,

I'll appreciate

But what can you offer this woman,

After a high priced date?

Before you approach me,

With silver tongued phrases

Play with my heart and put me through paces

Answer the question man:

Can you move me?

MY ONLY NEED

LET ME BE THE PUZZLE PIECE,

THAT FITS AND COMPLETES.

LET ME BE YOUR SUGAR

THAT MAKES THIS LOVE SWEET.

MY ONLY NEED

I want to be more than your desire.
Let me be your next breath.
Not a fleeting moment,
but through life until death.

This love isn't passing,
it's anchored and staying,
passionate, endless, invigorating.

Let me be the puzzle piece,
that fits and completes.
Let me be the sugar
that makes this love sweet.

Let me be the air,
that gives lift to your wings.
Let me be the melodious song
your heart longs to sing.

To be all that to you, my love;
is my only need.
Come, partake of my love
and allow yourself to be freed.

PAINT MYSELF GOLD

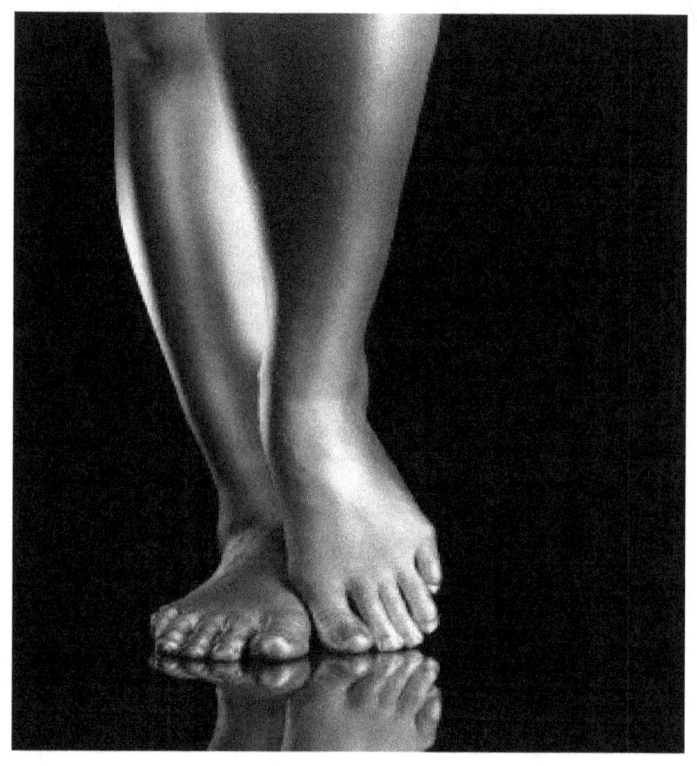

I WOULD PAINT MYSELF GOLD
IF IT MEANT YOU WOULD NOTICE ME.
I'M JUST A POOR CHILD
LIVING IN THE LAND OF OPPORTUNITY.

PAINT MYSELF GOLD

I would paint myself gold
if it meant you would notice me.
I'm just a poor child
living in the Land of Opportunity.

Mommy works so hard,
but makes very little money.
We have no light or heat
My family lives in poverty.

I rush to do my homework,
before night-time falls.
That's when the drug dealers come out
and begin their street battles.

All the shooting scares me.
I want a safer home.
They fight for a piece of concrete
that they will never own.

Police are on every corner,
I don't think they care for me,
because all day long
they fight what my future could be.

(Continued)

PAINT MYSELF GOLD

I look forward to the holidays,
Thanksgiving and Christmas feasts,
that's the one time of year
we always have plenty to eat.

We get big gifts,
new shoes, clothes and toys.
Even Mommy gets new things.
That fills my heart with joy.

I wish I could be a superhero
and protect my family and friends.
I'd beat up all the drug dealers
so the streets would be safe again.

There are a lot of families like mine
living in my neighborhood,
we are poor, but hope hard and pray
that our lives will turn out good.

When I look at all my neighbors,
I wonder again and again,
if I painted us all gold,
would you notice us then?

PAINT MYSELF GOLD

I would paint myself gold
if it meant you would notice me.
I'm just a poor child
living in the Land of Opportunity.

Mommy works so hard,
but makes very little money.
We have no light or heat
My family lives in poverty.

I rush to do my homework,
before night-time falls.
That's when the drug dealers come out
and begin their street battles.

All the shooting scares me.
I want a safer home.
They fight for a piece of concrete
that they will never own.

Police are on every corner,
I don't think they care for me,
because all day long
they fight what my future could be.

(Continued)

PAINT MYSELF GOLD

I look forward to the holidays,
Thanksgiving and Christmas feasts,
that's the one time of year
we always have plenty to eat.

We get big gifts,
new shoes, clothes and toys.
Even Mommy gets new things.
That fills my heart with joy.

I wish I could be a superhero
and protect my family and friends.
I'd beat up all the drug dealers
so the streets would be safe again.

There are a lot of families like mine
living in my neighborhood,
we are poor, but hope hard and pray
that our lives will turn out good.

When I look at all my neighbors,
I wonder again and again,
if I painted us all gold,
would you notice us then?

PERSISTENCE OF VISION

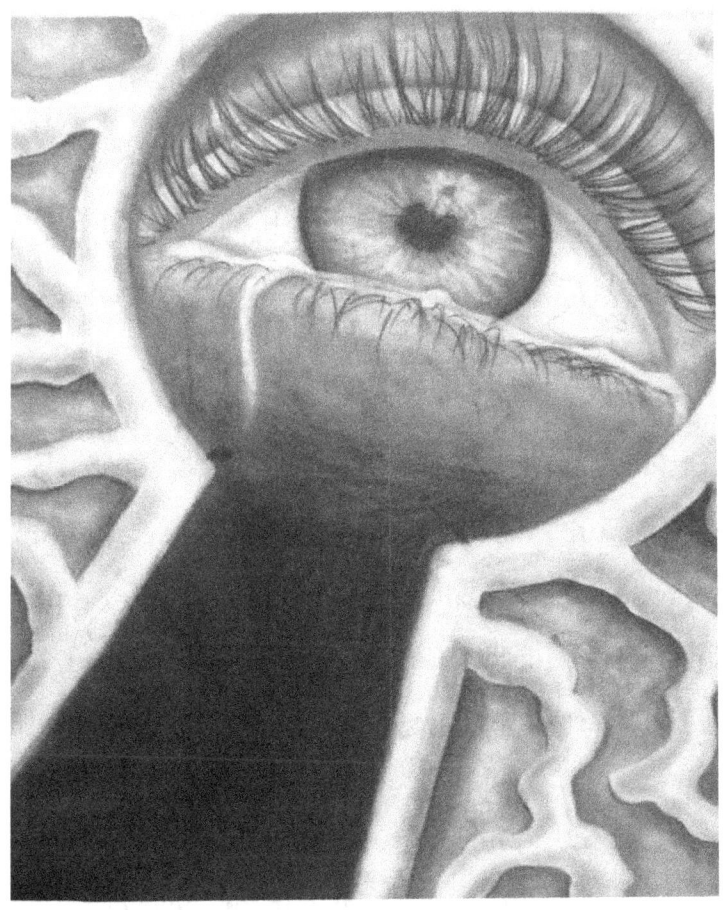

STILL, AN IMAGE WON'T FIT IN A FRAME.
SOME THINGS ARE ONLY MEANT FOR THE EYES.

PERSISTENCE OF VISION

The soul gets lost when you try to still time.
Modern technology can't do the moment justice.
Some things are only meant for the eyes to receive.

The memory serves as the best recorder.
It's a broad canvas that establishes the scenes,
in proper emotional perspective.

Pictures, moving and still have their place.
They coax the memory, which has been buried in time,
to awaken and recall every movement and sound,
and smell and emotion, so the soul can be stirred
and the heart can be moved by the image once more.

Still, an image won't fit in a frame.
Some things are only meant for the eyes.

RIGHT HERE

BUT WHAT ABOUT THE UNCERTAINTY

WHEN THE EMOTIONS,

EBB AND FLOW LIKE THE WATERS OF THE SEA?

RIGHT HERE

You are here and then gone again
too busy to be still or maybe it's fear.
But what do you have to fear of me, Dear one?

What is it that makes you flee,
and then again return to me?
Unsettled soul be still, be free
So I can be with you and you with me.

Wait….

Maybe it was never meant to be.
They say if you turn a thing loose, you set it free;
and if it comes back it belongs to thee.
But what about the uncertainty when the emotions,
ebb and flow like the waters of the sea?

Can the sea be tamed?
Though it pains me, Dear One,
it may be best if I let you go to find what you seek.
But know you can always find that place of peace
right here next to me.

ROSES AND THORNS

(Benedita da Silva)

NONE OF US STARTED OUT AS MUCH.
WE WERE ALL SEEDS, SAME SHAPE AND SIZE.
BUT WHEN WE GROW TOGETHER,
AND OUR BRANCHES REACH TOWARDS EACH OTHER
WE ARE AN IMPENETRABLE FORCE.
NOTHING CAN BREAK US DOWN.

ROSES AND THORNS

(Benedita da Silva)

I didn't start out as much.

I was barely a thought,

scarcely a hope.

But know this: I am a rose, I am also a thorn.

My skin is dark, so they call me ugly,

but when I open my mouth

they discover where my true beauty lies.

When I speak, they discover my fragrance.

When they mistreat me they discover the lioness within.

My passion is for my people,

those that are treated like they are invisible.

Our lives are intertwined; an unbreakable chain.

None of us started out as much.

We were all seeds, same shape and size.

But when we grow together,

and our branches reach towards each other.

We are an impenetrable force.

Nothing can break us down.

(Continued)

ROSES AND THORNS

(Benedita da Silva)

When the sun sets,
the words of the adversaries will whither and fade,
but the evidence of our work will forever remain.

We didn't start out as much.
We were barely a thought,
scarcely a hope.
But know this: We are the rose.
We are also the thorn.

BENEDITA SOUZA DA SILVA SAMPAIO

Benedita Souza da Silva Sampaio, was born on April 26, 1943 in Praia do Pinto, in Rio de Janeiro to Ovidia da Silva out of wedlock, despite the fact that Ovidia was married to someone other than Benedita's father. Her mother later revealed to Benedita who her real father was. She is one of Ovidia's 13 children. Benedita da Silva is also known as Bene' and is an African-Brazilian politician. Throughout her life, Benedita faced prejudice and racism for her humble and African origins, but she has overcome those barriers by becoming the first female and black governor of the state of Rio de Janeiro. Moreover, President Luiz Inacio Lula da Silva nominated her Secretary of State as well.

More about Bene here: http://en.wikipedia.org/wiki/Benedita_da_Silva
http://www.iwasbornablackwoman.com/

OASIS

You were here.

Your presence was refreshing

like an oasis in the desert.

Your touch was tender.

Your voice soft and deep

reached the inner most part of me.

You smelled of sandalwood

and vetiver, warm and sweet,

and just as I was about to taste your lips

you vanished

like vapor.

I opened my eyes.

Reality set in.

It was all a dream.

Oh, how I hate to dream.

SATISFACTION

WHO LOVES YA BABY?

IT'S A RHETORICAL QUESTION.

I SMILE BECAUSE I JUST DISCOVERED THE ANSWER.

IT'S MY OWN LITTLE SECRET.

MY VERY OWN POT OF GOLD.

SATISFACTION

Who loves Ya Baby?

It's a rhetorical question.

I smile because I just discovered the answer.

It's my own little secret.

My very own pot of gold.

Everyone knows we are part of each other.

We belong to each other.

He calls me His,

and He is all mine.

He covers and protects me,

before I ever ask.

After every heartbreak, He was there.

He caught every tear drop.

When I fell,

He was my soft landing.

I walked away; He waited for me to return.

It feels good to be loved like this.

SHE

What began as exploratory curiosity
eventually led to a single rendezvous
in a room hidden from the light of day,
but quickly turned into frequent assignations,
and innumerable stolen moments
of explosive passion and lust;
only to abruptly end with final breaths of regret.

If She gave too much,
he took more than his share
and demanded more still to feed his ego's insatiable
appetite for her tender flesh.
Shameless suppliant, foolish guttersnipe!
She bathed him with amorous words
and lofty immemorial fantasies
of him being Her first and evermore immorato
and Her being The One his soul longs for.
Yet, was not his soul, but his loins alone
that longed for Her.

(Continued)

SHE

She believed his lies of the time being too soon
and his desire to know
Her deepest thoughts and emotions
before he could present Her as his crowned jewel
until She saw him in the arms of another
who did not love him as well as She.
But he courted her and presented her to all he knew
and flaunted her as though she were new to the world.

But she wasn't worthy,
There was no way she knew how to speak to his soul
as She had done in their clandestine encounters.

Could She be so easily replaced?
Truth settled in Her heart and shattered its walls.
He was never Hers and never intended to be.
So, She went back to their hiding place,
and cried over the cessation of his attention
and welcomed Quietus as if it were
Her next romantic pursuit and clung to it
wishing it was he taking Her to rest.

SUSTAIN

THE MUSICAL BREEZE CAUSED HIM TO SWAY LIKE A FIELD OF GRASS AS HE TOLD HIS STORY, **WITHOUT SAYING A WORD.**

SUSTAIN

With his eyes closed,
he chose to feel the melody
and listen to the subtly, the highs and lows,
the pitch and rolls and harmony
the cello and violin sang.

His muscular frame extended across the stage,
the flute punctuated his flight
the cymbal pronounced
his delicate dissent.

He told of pain and joy,
and sorrow, and love lost
then found again with every movement.

He took a breath,
and let the music flow through his soul.
He needed each note to sustain him,
so his spirit could flourish.
Arms raised, face relaxed,
the musical breeze caused him to sway
like a field of grass as he told his story,
without saying a word.

TESTIMONY

THE PREACHER TOLD MY BUSINESS,

AND I PRAISED THE LORD.

THE CONGREGATION HEARD MY STORY,

AND THEY PRAISED THE LORD.

TESTIMONY

The preacher told my business,
and I praised the Lord.
The congregation heard my story,
and they praised the Lord.

They nodded, danced and shouted,
as they praised the Lord.
They prayed and sang the Psalms,
as they praised the Lord.

They sang because there is hope for me,
and I praised the Lord.
The Holy Spirit swept across the room,
we all praised the Lord.

Slain saints were laid out on the floor,
and we praised the Lord.
Souls got saved, hands were raised,
in praise to the Lord.

The preacher told my business today,
I will praise the Lord.
Another soul will see The Gates,
for that, I praise the Lord.

THE DREAM IS YET ALIVE

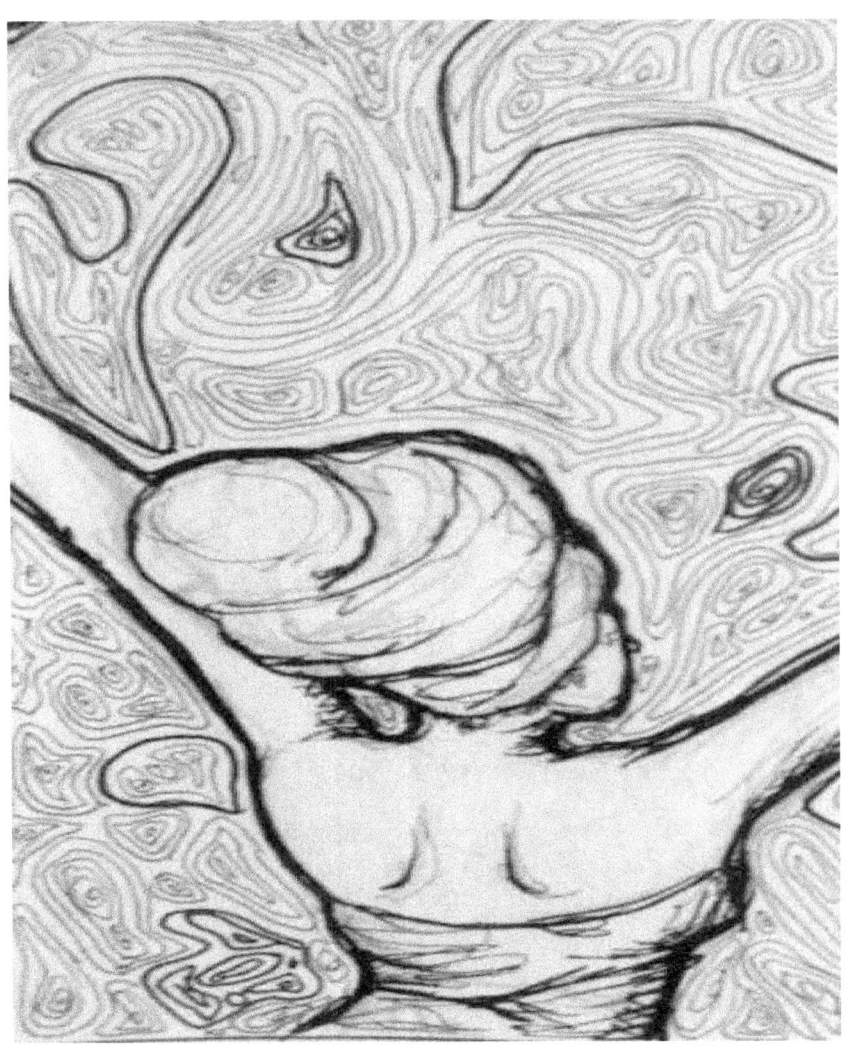

TO TELL THE GENERATIONS THAT FOLLOW,

THE DREAM IS YET ALIVE,

THE DREAM IS YET ALIVE.

THE DREAM IS YET ALIVE

Hope was given a voice.

Freedom declared

and reclaimed as our birthright.

Success required

for future generations.

Access expected to every opportunity.

Although the voice was silenced,

the echo can still be heard,

reverberating from the mountain tops.

His words,

Our legacy.

Our hope,

our responsibility

to tell the generations that follow,

The dream is yet alive,

The dream is yet alive.

THE MEASURE OF AN ARTIST

What will you sing about
when the money stops flowing?
Will you keep on singing?
Will you keep the music going?

What will you rap about
when the bling's gone dull?
When the booty gets old,
when all the clubs close?

What will you write about
when the ink well is dry?
When the graphite crumbles,
will you even try?

When the celluloid rots
and the colors fade,
when the themes run out
will your talent dissipate?

(Continued)

THE MEASURE OF AN ARTIST

When the actors gain integrity
and won't act out sex & violence,
will you believe working the arts
provide any benefit?

Have you thought about it?
Is your passion real?
Do you still have something to offer
if there is no deal?

Will you hide your offering?
Or
Will you sing?
Will you write?
Will you rap?
Will you act?
Will you give?
Will you? Will you?

WHAT YOU SEE BEFORE YOU

What you see before you
is a woman complete.
A "better-half" is not required
to increase my value.

A whole man with a vision
is what I desire.
Seeking a mate is not my duty,
but a wise man's position.

Integrity and imagination,
sound spirit and love of God
are the treasures I possess.
If you believe you are my equal,
then extend the invitation.

Two whole people becoming one,
in mind, body and spirit,
with God as the center
is true perfection.
The choice is before you brother,
make the right selection.

YOU ARE NOBODY

Before sex, don't you want to be loved?

After sex don't you want to be loved?

Somewhere along the way

you confused the physical

for the emotional;

the moment,

for forever.

Sometimes the intangible

is more valuable.

You dabble in the art of romance

or so you think.

Soft music, candlelight,

sugar sweet words whispered

as you caress her naked skin.

You believe that because you know

how to create the atmosphere,

and how to lay it down,

and make that woman

scream your name,

or coo like a dove

that you are a master lover.

(Continued)

YOU ARE NOBODY

But don't you know

that even if you dwell

forever in her secret place,

your ability to stroke

her double and triple time

is not enough to make her love you?

You must know

after all is said and done

that you are nobody

until somebody loves you.

ABOUT THE AUTHOR

Nike Binger Marshall

Nike Binger Marshall was born in Brooklyn, NY. She enjoys watching, and often draws inspiration for her poetry from documentaries and sharing little known black history facts on her blogs. After a long break from writing, she revisited her passion for writing in 2004 and has been writing ever since. She is one of the winners of the 2008 Delaware Art Museum's Eye/I Witness Gordon Parks contest. Nike currently lives in Wilmington, DE with her daughter Zeni.

Visit Nike's blog at http://nikewrites.wordpress.com

CONTRIBUTING ARTIST

Kayla Stern

Kayla Stern was born in Newark, Delaware. She is a recent graduate of Middletown High School, was a member of the National Honor's Society and currently attends Delaware College of Art and Design. In her free time she enjoys watching old movies and reading African American literature.

Kayla's artistry is displayed on page 33 for the Persistence of Vision poem and on page 49 for the Dream is Yet Alive poem.

PERSISTENCE OF VISION TELECOM DEFINITION

The theory that electrochemical processing delays in the human eye or human brain create the illusion of continuity of motion if a series of images is presented in rapid succession. The theory is based on the discoveries of Paul Nipkow, a German engineer who developed the first true television mechanism in 1884. Nipkow used a scanning disk, lenses, mirrors, a selenium cell, and electrical conductors to transmit images in rapid succession to a lamp that changed in brightness according to the strength of the currents received. Using this mechanical scanning technique, Nipkow demonstrated that portions of a full image viewed in rapid succession created the illusion of viewing the full image. It later was discovered that viewing 15 or more images per second created the illusion of full motion.

Site: "persistence of vision." <u>Webster's New World Telecom Dictionary</u>. 2009 Your Dictionary. 20 March 2009 <www.yourdictionary.com/telecom/persistence-of-vision>

www.ingramcontent.com/pod-product-compliance
Lightning Source LLC
Chambersburg PA
CBHW071842290426
44109CB00017B/1901